There's No One Like You, Snoopy

Charles M. Schulz

Selected Cartoons from
You're You, Charlie Brown Vol. 2

CORONET BOOKS
Hodder Fawcett, London

Copyright © 1967, 1968 by United
Feature Syndicate Inc.

First Published by Fawcett Publications Inc.,
New York 1973

Coronet Edition 1974
Seventh impression 1978

Printed in Great Britain for
Hodder Fawcett Ltd., Mill Road, Dunton Green,
Sevenoaks, Kent (Editorial Office:
47 Bedford Square, London WC1 3DP) by
C. Nicholls & Company Ltd,
The Philips Park Press, Manchester

ISBN 0 340 18303 9

IS THIS YOUR BAT, CHARLIE BROWN? IT DOESN'T HAVE YOUR NAME ON IT...

YOU SHOULD HAVE YOUR NAME ON YOURS LIKE ALL OF THE BIG LEAGUE PLAYERS

LINUS HAS A WOOD-BURNING SET AT HOME...WHY DON'T I TAKE YOUR BAT, AND PUT YOUR NAME ON IT?

..AND WE FOUND YOUR CAP OVER TWO BLOCKS AWAY, AND ONE OF YOUR SHOES THREE BLOCKS AWAY, AND ONE OF YOUR SOCKS TWO BLOCKS AWAY, AND..

ALL RIGHT!

POW!

SCHULZ

THAT'S AN INTERESTING
POINT OF VIEW...

HOW SHALL WE PITCH THIS NEXT GUY, CHARLIE BROWN?

WELL, I DON'T KNOW..

THROW HIM YOUR CURVE, CHARLIE BROWN

SAY, HAVE YOU NOTICED HOW BUILT-UP IT'S GETTING AROUND HERE? PRETTY SOON THERE WON'T BE ANY PLACE FOR US TO PLAY...LOOK AT ALL THE HOUSES...

MY GRAMPA SAYS THAT ALL OF THIS USED TO BE A BIG PASTURE..

AS I CLIMB INTO THE SKY, THE HUGE Le Rhône ROTARY ENGINE IN MY SOPWITH CAMEL THROBS ITS SONG OF DESTINY!

WE FLYING ACES ARE VERY DRAMATIC

MY MISSION IS TO FLY SOUTH FROM VERDUN TO ST. MIHIEL AND THEN SOUTHWEST TO BAR-LE-DUC, HOPING TO TRAP A GERMAN GOTHA BOMBER IN THE NIGHT...

THERE'S ONLY ONE THING WRONG...

BAM BAM BAM BAM

I'M AFRAID OF THE DARK!

SNOW?!
BUT I'M NOT READY FOR WINTER!
MY BLOOD'S TOO THIN! I STILL HAVE MY SUMMER FUR!
STOP SNOWING! STOP IT, I SAY! STOP THIS STUPID SNOWING!
RATS!
SCHULZ

I KNOW WHAT'S ON YOUR MIND...

LET ME WARN YOU RIGHT NOW THAT FOR EVERY SNOWBALL YOU THROW AT ME, I'M GOING TO CLOBBER YOU WITH *FIVE!*

WAP!

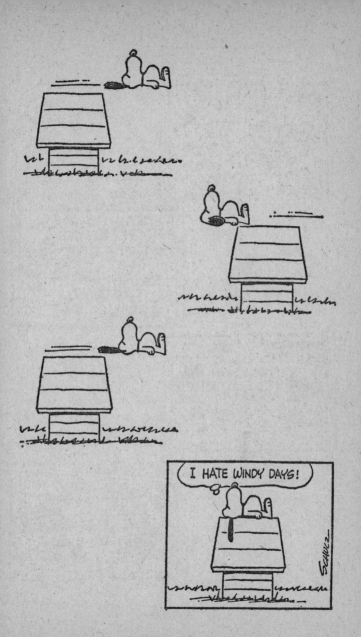

REAL FIGURE SKATERS SMILE A LOT...

MAYBE JUST A PLEASANT GRIN WOULD BE BETTER..

→

And don't forget about all the other PEANUTS books in CORONET Book editions. Good Grief! More than FIVE MILLION of them in paperback! See the check-list overleaf.

© 1970 United Feature Syndicate, Inc.

Wherever Paperbacks Are Sold

THE LATEST PEANUTS

All these books are available at your local bookshop or newsagent, or can be ordered direct from the publisher. Just tick the titles you want and fill in the form below.
Prices and availability subject to change without notice.

CORONET BOOKS, P.O. Box 11, Falmouth, Cornwall.
Please send cheque or postal order, and allow the following for postage and packing:
U.K. – One book 22p plus 10p per copy for each additional book ordered, up to a maximum of 82p.
B.F.P.O. and EIRE – 22p for the first book plus 10p per copy for the next 6 books, thereafter 4p per book.
OTHER OVERSEAS CUSTOMERS – 30p for the first book and 10p per copy for each additional book.

Name...

Address...

....